Page Turners

The Stranger

Andrew Watson

T0308190

Series Editor: Rob Waring
Story Editor: Julian Thomlinson
Series Development Editor: Sue Leather

HEINLE
CENGAGE Learning™

Australia • Brazil • Japan • Korea • Mexico • Singapore • Spain • United Kingdom • United States

HEINLE
CENGAGE Learning™

Page Turners Reading Library

The Stranger
Andrew Watson

Publisher: Andrew Robinson

Executive Editor: Sean Bermingham

Associate Development Editor:
Sarah Tan

Director of Global Marketing:
Ian Martin

Content Project Manager:
Tan Jin Hock

Senior Print Buyer:
Mary Beth Hennebury

Layout Design and Illustrations:
Redbean Design Pte Ltd

Cover Illustration: Eric Foenander

Photo Credits:
76 Photos.com

Library of Congress Control Number: 2011931827
ISBN-13: 978-1-4240-4892-2
ISBN-10: 1-4240-4892-3

Heinle
20 Channel Center Street
Boston, Massachusetts 02210
USA

Cengage Learning is a leading provider of customized learning solutions with office locations around the globe, including Singapore, the United Kingdom, Australia, Mexico, Brazil, and Japan. Locate your local office at:
international.cengage.com/region

Cengage Learning products are represented in Canada by Nelson Education, Ltd.

Visit Heinle online at **elt.heinle.com**

Visit our corporate website at **www.cengage.com**

Printed in the United States of America
1 2 3 4 5 6 7 – 15 14 13 12 11

Contents

BELLA ANNA

People in the story

Anna Cross
delivers the mail in the
village of Kilverbeg

Callum McKendry
a secretive visitor
to Kilverbeg

Stuart Cross
Anna's father, a fisherman

Donald Ferguson
Kilverbeg's local
policeman

The story is set in Kilverbeg, a small village in Scotland.

Chapter 1

The beginning

He arrived in Kilverbeg on a Tuesday; in our village it's easy to remember when something exciting happens.

"He must be about your age, Anna," said Mrs. Black. That was the first thing she said to me when I stepped into her shop. "He can't be more than twenty-five, anyway."

"Who?"

"Haven't you heard?"

"Heard what?"

Mrs. Black walked round from behind the fruit and vegetable display, shaking her head in wonder. She must have thought I had nothing better to do than stand around in the Post Office like everyone else and listen to the talk.

"He's rented my flat! I tell you, Anna, after almost eighteen months, it's a relief to have someone in there. The place isn't the way it was. It's the sea air, you see. It makes everything damp. It's even affected the lock. Honestly, it was embarrassing. I had to ask him to open the door for me, it was so stuck. But he's still paid for a month, and in cash. And if he likes it here, he said he might stay longer."

I tried again, louder this time. "Who? I don't know who you're talking about!"

Mrs. Black picked up an apple from her display and began to wipe it with a cloth. "Callum, that's his name. Callum something. I wrote it down somewhere." She waved the cloth in the air. "But really, I don't mind who he is. As long as he pays his rent, I don't mind at all."

"And he's come to live here? In Kilverbeg?!"

"Why is that so surprising?"

"Well . . ." I began. Like most people in the village, Mrs. Black's family had lived in the area for generations. I didn't want to upset her by being rude about the place. Perhaps she liked living a boring life. "There's no work here, is there?"

Happy with her display, Mrs. Black walked back behind the counter. "Maybe he's not looking for work. Maybe he's brought his work with him. Perhaps he's an artist, or a photographer. Maybe he's writing a book. Whatever he's doing, he's got money to pay the rent. That's all I know."

"But didn't you ask him?"

"He just said Kilverbeg looked like a nice place to stay for a while. And I'm not going to argue with that, am I?"

I didn't reply. I just put her mail down on the counter.

"What have you got for me today?" she asked.

"Just a few bills, and your local paper."

"What does it say? Any interesting news?"

"Just the usual," I pointed to the newspaper's front page. "Andy's bus stopped on the hill again. He and Mrs. MacPatrick had to wait three hours for the recovery truck from Fort Angus. And there's another story about the old pier."

Mrs. Black put on her glasses and stared at the newspaper. "What are they saying about that now?"

"That it's time to pull it down. It's old and no one uses it anymore. Although if that was a reason for pulling things down, we'd have to destroy half the village."

Mrs. Black looked at me carefully. She couldn't tell if I was being serious. Finally she laughed. "Oh, Anna! You are funny!"

"I'll see you later, Mrs. Black. I've got to get on."

"If you see that man Callum, be nice to him," she called, as I walked out of the shop. "Make sure he knows he can stay as long as he wants."

I waved through the window in reply, then checked in my bag—a letter for Mrs. Grant at number four, and a parcel for Mrs. MacKenzie at number twelve. With a quick look to see if it was going to rain, I began to walk up the High Street.

I don't know why it's called the High Street. It's really Kilverbeg's only street. And of the nine shops, two of them were closed and empty. Mr. Green, who used to run the fish shop, gave up at last three years before, and retired to Glasgow. And one of my few friends still left in the village, Heather Farmer, the hairdresser, had closed her shop the previous year and gone to have babies in Inverness.

Kilverbeg was slowly dying. When the fishing industry was strong, almost eight hundred people lived across the area. Now there were less than five hundred, and that number was growing older and smaller every year. No one new had moved to Kilverbeg in many years.

So of all the places in all the world, why had this stranger come here?

I knocked quietly on his door and waited. The longer I waited, the more nervous I became. After all, I didn't have any post to give him. Simple curiosity had made me stop as I was driving past. I was as bad as all the old women in the Post Office after all.

The thought made me feel slightly ashamed, so I turned back toward the van to continue my deliveries. And that's when I heard him trying to open the door. I waited while he struggled with the lock, until at last his head appeared around the side.

"Yes?" he said.

That first time I saw him, I thought that Mrs. Black had been wrong. He looked much older than I, perhaps as much as thirty. With those dark eyes on me, I certainly felt a lot younger.

"I'm sorry to bother you," I said, feeling uncomfortable as I walked back toward him. "My name's Anna. I work for the Post Office." I pointed at the red van parked by the road and he nodded. "I just heard that you've moved to Kilverbeg and I wanted to say hello, to welcome you."

He looked surprised. And then, without opening his door any wider, he stepped out onto the street. He was wearing an old pair of jeans and a sweater. It didn't look very clean. "Anna?" he repeated, looking down at me. He was very tall.

"That's right. I live down beyond the church."

At last, he held out his hand and smiled. It was a smile that changed his face, and made him look hardly any older than I. "It's good to meet you," he said. "My name's Callum. Or Cal."

I smiled in reply and shook his hand. It was like one of my dad's hands; the skin was hard and rough.

"It was nice of you to stop by," he said. His voice was deep, and his accent strong like mine.

"How's the flat?" I asked, looking over his shoulder at the darkness beyond. "Not too damp, I hope? It's been empty a while."

"It'll do me just fine."

"Good." Of course, I wanted to ask what he was doing in Kilverbeg, and he knew it. He just stood there, smiling and waiting for me to ask. And so I didn't.

"Have you been to Kilverbeg before?" I asked instead.

"Never."

"It won't take you long to find your way about. Do you know Argyll at all?"

"I've never been further west than Glasgow."

"Did you live in Glasgow?"

"For a while," Cal nodded.

"I'd love to live in Glasgow. I visit when I can. I've a few friends who live near the Byres Road. Do you know it?"

"I do."

"It's an interesting exchange you've made, Kilverbeg for Glasgow."

He nodded, still smiling. "They're quite different, it's true."

"*Quite* different?" I laughed. "You mean like a swimming pool is 'quite different' to the Atlantic Ocean?"

Cal's smile grew wider as he nodded. But he said nothing.

For a brief moment, we stood in silence, each of us waiting for the other to speak. And then I gave in.

"Well, I have to get going. I only stopped to say hello and see if there's anything you need . . ."

"I'm doing fine, thank you, Anna."

"You're welcome. I can say with confidence that I'll see you later. It's not like Glasgow here." I smiled. "It's 'quite different.'"

Without waiting for a reply, I climbed into the van and began to drive away. And it surprised me how tempted I was to turn and look back. I wanted to see whether he was watching me leave.

Chapter 2

The last fisherman

In fact, I saw Cal again only a few hours later. I was down by the harbor. It was a typical west coast summer day. The sun was trying to show its face just once before the evening came, but the clouds weren't going to let it through.

It wasn't actually raining. But from the look on Cal's face, it might have been. He was sitting on the rails that lined the road, not moving. And his eyes were fixed on a faraway part of the sea.

"You're not regretting coming here already, are you?" I asked, trying to make a joke.

Cal looked up. There was sadness in his eyes.

"You look the way I feel when my dad starts singing," I told him.

He didn't smile. "I think it's going to rain," he said.

I stopped beside him and stood against the rails. "If it's rain that makes you so sad, you're going to be miserable in Kilverbeg."

At last, he smiled. "You've finished work?"

"Yeah. And you're settled into the flat?"

"I think so, thanks."

There was a silence as we both stared out to sea.

"OK," I said, turning to him at last. "I give in. Tell me."

"Tell you what?"

"You know perfectly well. Tell me what you're doing in Kilverbeg."

Cal stood up and pushed his hands into his pockets. Now he looked like he was trying not to smile. "What do you think I'm doing in Kilverbeg?"

"I've no idea. But I can guarantee that everyone in the Hope is asking the same question."

"The Hope?"

I pointed past the lifeboat station to the building a little farther along the beach. "The Hope and Anchor. Our local pub."

"Oh."

"Well?"

He ran a hand through his hair. It was thick and black, and obviously hadn't been cut in months. "The truth is," he said, "I don't really know what I'm doing here. I just decided to do a little traveling. And since I don't know this part of Scotland at all, it seemed a good place to visit."

"So you're just traveling around the country?"

"That's right. I've no family and no job, so why not?"

"No reason at all. I think it's a great idea. I'd do the same, if I could."

"And why can't you?"

"Maybe someday I will. At least, I hope so. But for the moment, I'm stuck in Kilverbeg. My dad's not getting any younger, and he's not got anyone else to look after him. So the most I'm likely to see of the wide world will be on the postcards and magazines I have to deliver."

"That must be difficult for you," said Cal. "But family's important."

"I guess so." I looked back out to sea, to where the clouds were now dropping their rain on the islands to the west. "So how do you pay for your travels?" I asked. "Are you rich?"

Cal smiled and shook his head. "Would I dress like this if I was rich?"

I looked at his old jacket. There were lines of mud on it and one of the sleeves was torn. It looked like he'd borrowed it from someone even bigger than him.

"I guess not," I said.

"I take what work I can find along the way."

"You'll be lucky to find anything here. If it's work you want, you have to go back to Glasgow, or at least to Fort Angus. It used to be the fishing that kept Kilverbeg alive. When I was a girl, I could pull a single line behind a boat in the bay there and in less than an hour I would catch enough to feed two families. Now I'd be lucky to catch an old boot."

"Are there no fishing boats working out of here anymore?"

"Just that one." I pointed to where a boat was entering the bay. A cloud of birds was following it home, each one hoping to steal some of the catch.

Cal raised a hand against the evening light. "He seems to have had a good day."

"That boat brings home more fish than any other in Argyll. That's the only reason it's still working. All the other local boats were sold years ago. It's got the best captain on the west coast. But he still has to work hard. He's out most of the day, and sometimes through the night."

"So he's the last fisherman in Kilverbeg?" asked Cal. He began walking toward the harbor.

"That's right," I said, following. "The only one. For the last four years at least."

The boat was coming closer. It was near enough to see the captain behind the wheel, and the cigarette in his mouth.

"He looks like a fisherman," said Cal.

I laughed. "What does that mean? What should a fisherman look like?"

"I don't know. Like he could go on forever, whatever the weather. Like he's stared into a thousand storms, and could stare into a thousand more."

I laughed. "Not him. I don't think he could manage another hundred storms. Not if he keeps smoking like he does."

"You know him?"

"Of course, and not just because everyone here knows everyone else. That's my dad."

Chapter 3

The *Bella Anna*

With the boat safely tied up, Dad pulled off his gloves and threw his cigarette into the sea. He knew what I thought of his smoking.

"A good day?" I asked.

"Good enough," he smiled, bending to kiss me. "And you?"

"Not too bad. Dad, this is Cal. I would tell you his last name, but he likes a bit of mystery."

"There's no mystery, Mr. Cross. It's Mackendry. Callum Mackendry."

"Call me Stuart," said Dad, and the two men shook hands.

"Wait a minute," I smiled, turning to Cal. "How do you know our last name is Cross? I never told you that."

Cal looked down at me and returned the smile. "Kilverbeg's a small place, isn't it? Are you going to tell me there's more than one Anna here who delivers the mail?"

Obviously Cal had been asking about me in the village. I tried to stop myself smiling further. "It is a small place," I agreed. "And people talk too much."

"And you're no different to them," said Dad. "Come on! Let's get the boat unloaded."

"Can I help?" asked Cal.

"If you don't mind the sight of dead fish," Dad laughed, "we'd be happy to have your help."

Twenty minutes later, the day's catch was unloaded.

"What happens to them now?" asked Cal, pointing at the two dozen full fish boxes waiting by the roadside.

"There's a van that will collect them. I'll give the driver a call and soon those fish will be packed in ice and on the road. They'll be on someone's breakfast plate in Glasgow by the morning."

"So where do you find all the fish? I hear the waters around here are nearly empty."

"That's true," nodded Dad. Then he smiled. "But there are still a few out there, if you know where to look."

"And that must be your satellite recorder," said Cal. He pointed to a small white box beside the radio, attached to the inside of the boat.

"How do you know that?" I asked, surprised.

"I used to do a little fishing myself."

"That's the way the industry is now, I'm afraid," said Dad. "They're making it harder and harder for us to make a living. When I started fishing, I never thought we would have satellites recording every movement. Next they'll tell us we can't go to sea without a policeman to measure every fish we catch."

Cal laughed politely and walked the length of the boat. "The *Bella Anna*," he said, reading the name on its side. "It's a fine-looking ship. Have you had it long?"

"I bought it soon after Anna was born, and named it after her. Back in 1990."

Cal turned to face me and smiled. "I'd say they've both aged well." Then, fortunately before he could see my embarrassment, he turned back to the boat. "It looks almost new."

"That's because a lot of it *is* new, especially around the front," I said. Dad was looking uncomfortable, which made me laugh. "A couple of years ago, he was setting out for a day's work and sailed straight into the harbor wall. It's solid stone, so the boat wasn't too happy. I had the fun of pulling him back into harbor behind the lifeboat."

"You work on the lifeboat?" asked Cal. I could see that he was impressed.

"Someone has to," I said. "But I wasn't the only one who saw the poor *Bella Anna* pulled home. Most of the village was standing on the harbor and watching."

"Alright, Anna," smiled Dad. "I don't need you to remind me of it. And what about you, Cal? What brings you to Kilverbeg?"

"I'm just passing through. I'm traveling around the west coast, seeing a bit of the country."

Dad pulled another cigarette out of a box in his pocket, and put it in his mouth. "That sounds like a fun summer," he said, lighting it.

"I hope so."

"Well, I'm sure I'll see you again before you go. For the moment, though, you'll have to excuse me. I've got to finish up and get changed." He turned toward his small office on the edge of the harbor. "Thanks again for your help."

"You're welcome," said Cal. "And I've got to get home myself. It's been good to meet you. And good to see you again, Anna."

"Good night," I replied, and he walked away.

"A good-looking boy," said Dad. It was only then that I realized I was still staring after Cal.

"I suppose so," I said.

"Come on, Anna," he smiled. "Don't pretend you're not interested. I saw the way you looked at him."

"Would that be so terrible?"

"You only met him this morning! And he said it himself: he's only passing through."

At that moment, a police car approached the harbor.

Dad nodded toward it. "Now that's someone you *should* be interested in. You're making Donald miserable, you know."

I gave Dad a look. "Donald is great, but he's just a friend, Dad. You know that."

"Well, be nice to him," he said, shaking his head with a smile. "Don't go making an enemy of our local policeman or we'll both be in trouble!"

With a wave to Donald, who was now walking toward me, Dad disappeared into his office.

"Anna!" shouted Donald. "I thought I'd find you here. A good catch?"

"Not bad," I said, closing my jacket against the growing wind.

He shook his head in admiration. "I don't know how your dad does it." There was something a bit sad about his words. Donald's dad had been a fisherman, too. But the lack of fish forced him to retire early.

"I was wondering if you fancy a quick drink in the Hope?" he said. "It's quiz night. I thought we could make up a team?"

"That's a nice idea, Donald," I replied. The two of us often joined in the quiz nights in the Hope and Anchor. It was a popular competition. "But I've just promised my dad I'll cook him his dinner."

"Are you sure? I could do with your help. I'm awful at those geography questions, and you always get them right."

"I'm sorry. We're just about to leave for home."

Donald nodded. "OK," he said, still quite cheerful. "Maybe another time?"

"Sure," I said. "Another time."

BELLA ANNA

He stood for a moment like he was wondering what to say next. The wind blew some of his red hair into his eyes and he brushed it away. "Have a good night, then," he said. "Maybe I'll see you tomorrow."

"Good night, Donald," I said, and watched him walk back to his car. I wondered if I was being mean. After all, I liked Donald. I'd known him almost all my life. We were in the same class together. And he was the only other person from that class still in Kilverbeg.

But we were different, in an important way. He never seemed to think about the world beyond the village, while I couldn't think of much else. No one else in Kilverbeg seemed to understand that. Except Cal.

Chapter 4

Fort Angus

I don't know what Cal was doing for the rest of that week. There was no mail for him so I had nothing to deliver, but I tried knocking on his door a few times anyway as I passed his flat. There was never any answer. And although I looked, I never saw him around the village.

That Saturday morning, I was sitting in the back of the bus, waiting to leave for the usual weekly shop. Fort Angus is only thirty miles away, but the road is very slow. It takes over an hour to get there. And it takes even longer when the bus is having problems.

Andy Bruce was the driver. I used to go to school with his daughter, Linda. She was now a prison guard in Glasgow. I still stayed with her every few months. Andy and I were just waiting for Mr. and Mrs. Galbraith—they were always slow getting ready—when Cal climbed inside. I was about to call to him but then, as he saw me, he seemed to hesitate. It really looked like he might turn around and step off the bus again. At that moment, Mrs. Galbraith arrived at last and started climbing up behind him. Unable to go back, Cal was forced to continue forward toward me, but by that time he was smiling.

"Anna!" he said, as though he was noticing me for the first time.

I only nodded.

"Do you mind if I sit with you?" he asked.

"If you want. Although I don't think this bus has ever been full. There are plenty of other seats." I was being a bit childish, and I knew it. But I was genuinely hurt by his reaction.

"What's wrong?" he asked, looking down at me.

"You tell me. You didn't seem very happy to see me."

He looked puzzled, but then started laughing. "I'm sorry! It must have looked that way. But I thought for a minute that I had forgotten my wallet. I thought I'd miss the bus while I went back to get it. But then I remembered I put it in here." He held up a small shoulder bag. "Have you a long list of things to get?"

I shook my head. "Just the usual. My dad leaves all the shopping to me. Except for his cigarettes. I refuse to buy them for him."

"I don't blame you," nodded Cal. "So you don't mind if I sit down beside you?"

I felt foolish, and my face was growing red. I quickly shook my head again and turned toward the window.

Minutes later, we were on the way to Fort Angus. Mr. and Mrs. Galbraith sat up front, near Andy. Mr. Galbraith seemed happy to have Andy there; it gave him a chance to sleep while his wife talked to someone else. Otherwise the bus was empty, except for Cal and me.

Normally, the journey to Fort Angus is long and boring. The road runs past the same lochs and over the same hills that I've seen thousands of times before. I usually sit at the back with a book.

That day, though, it seemed to take us no more than ten minutes. And I never touched my book. By the time we stepped out at Fort Angus, I was aching from too much laughing. Cal and I talked and joked the whole way. I would have been happy if the journey was twice the distance. It was almost a disappointment to arrive.

"I'll help you with your shopping, if you like," said Cal. "I'm just going to see if I can get myself a new jacket. This one was my dad's. I think it's about time I got a replacement."

"Fine. Try the shop just up there," I said, pointing to Argyll Street. "Turn left at the corner. It's beside the chemist."

"Thanks. I'll meet you in the supermarket."

An hour later, Cal was lifting my shopping bags up into the bus, and Andy had started the engine, ready to return home. Mrs. Galbraith had already begun to chat to anyone who would listen, and I was just climbing in when I heard a voice.

"It *is* you!" I turned and saw an old woman hurrying toward Cal with a big smile. "I saw you in the Post Office and I *knew* it was you. How are you?"

Cal didn't reply. He just looked shocked, as though he didn't know what to say.

The old woman didn't notice his confusion. "I haven't seen you in so long," she continued breathlessly, but still smiling broadly. "It was just terrible what happened. I moved here to Fort Angus not long after. Where did you go?"

At last, Cal seemed to gain control of himself. "I'm sorry," he said. "You've made a mistake. We've never met before. Excuse me."

Without another word to the woman, he climbed quickly up into the bus and closed the door behind him. "Let's go," he said to Andy. "Before she decides she's my great aunt or something!"

With a little laugh, Andy started the bus and turned into the road.

"Did you hear that?" asked Cal, as he sat down beside me.

I nodded.

"That was pretty uncomfortable. Poor woman," he laughed. "She needs glasses. Or medicine."

"I guess so." I turned to look out the back window. The old woman was still standing by the roadside, watching us go. She looked hurt and confused.

"That's what happens when you've a face like mine," joked Cal. "It's too common. Everyone thinks they've seen me before."

"And you don't know her?"

"How could I? Unless . . ." he stopped.

"What?"

"I suppose there's a chance she knew me when I was much smaller. When I lived in Portrose."

"Portrose? On the east coast?"

"Right."

"I thought you said you lived in Glasgow?"

"I did, but not always. I grew up in Portrose."

"And that's where you fished? You said you'd done some fishing."

"That's right. My dad was a fisherman, too."

"If that's where your skills lie, it's no wonder you're out of work."

"I suppose you're right. But it's no joke. I've been in Kilverbeg almost a week, and I've found no work at all. If I can't find something soon, I'll have to look somewhere else. And that means I'll have to leave."

Chapter 5

The perfect solution?

I didn't talk much on the way home. Cal kept making jokes and talking happily, but I couldn't smile. It all seemed so unfair.

Dad had been right, of course. I was attracted to Cal. Knowing that he was in Kilverbeg, even during those days I hadn't seen him, had made the place a little brighter. Now that he was talking of leaving, and leaving to live the life that I wanted, I could already imagine how dark the village would seem without him.

We were almost home when I realized what the answer was.

"Of course!" I called, suddenly sitting up. "It's obvious!"

"What's obvious?" asked Cal.

"You need a job, right?"

"Yes."

"And you've worked on a fishing boat before?"

"That's right."

"So work for my dad!"

Cal shook his head. "You said that your dad has worked alone for years. He wouldn't want anyone else with him."

"He's sixty-two years old, and he's still working day and night! Sometimes he's gone for up to forty-eight hours, and miles away from the coast. He's not young anymore. He needs help."

"Do you really think he might agree?"

"The worst he can say is 'No.' He's home today. I'll ask him at lunch."

It took me over an hour to prepare Dad's favorite meal. And it took him less than five minutes to finish it. I didn't disturb him, but waited, carefully choosing the right time. Then, when his plate was empty, he sat back in his chair with a happy sigh, and I took a deep breath.

But before I could say anything, he spoke. "Alright, Anna," he said, "what is it you want?"

Of course, I pretended to be surprised. "What do you mean?"

"I know you, Anna. You don't cook me beef pie for lunch unless you're after something. So what is it?"

I shook my head. He knew me too well. "Dad, I've got a question."

With a knowing smile, he waited for me to speak.

"Maybe it's more of a suggestion." I picked up his empty plate and carried it through to the kitchen.

"What is it?" he called after me.

"I don't want you to get upset." I said, sitting down opposite him again. "But I think you should have some help on the boat, even if it's not every day. I'm worried that you're doing too much."

"Anna, I've been doing what I do every day of my adult life. Are you telling me I'm doing a bad job?"

"Not at all. I know that you can fish better than anyone alive. I'm just saying that you're not young anymore. And I worry about you. You work so hard. I think you deserve to make your life a little easier. You deserve some help."

"It's Cal, isn't it? You want me to give him some work."

"Cal is looking for work. He's going to have to leave if he can't find anything. And you heard him say it: he's got the right experience. He's young and he'd . . ."

"Half this village has the right experience," he interrupted. His voice was getting louder. "But there's a very good reason why they don't have the chance to use that experience. It's because the people who run this country have made so many rules and laws that there's no money in fishing anymore. So even if I wanted to, what makes you think I can afford to employ someone else? And what makes you think I would want to employ someone else to do a job I can manage quite happily on my own?"

Dad stood up. His face was starting to turn red.

"I appreciate that you're worried about me, Anna," he continued. "And you're right. I am getting older. But that doesn't mean I'm unable to do my job! Nor does it mean I've suddenly got money to spare to pay your boyfriend!"

"That's not fair, Dad. All I'm asking is that you think about it."

"I don't need to think about it," he shouted. "I'm not giving him any work."

"There's no shame in getting help. You're being too proud."

"And you're not being realistic. You want me to give money that we don't have to someone you barely know, for doing something I can do myself. You're not thinking straight. You're blind to your own feelings."

"And you're blind to your own age," I shouted back, before walking out of the house.

Dad and I don't often argue. Since Mum died, we've been a good team. But that day I felt so angry. It seemed to me that Dad had the chance to keep Cal in Kilverbeg. But he was deliberately choosing not to help.

Ten minutes later, I was knocking on Cal's door.

"He says he can't afford to employ anyone," I said, as soon as he opened it.

"You look angry."

"I *am* angry. We had an argument."

"I'm sorry to hear that. And I'm sorry to be the cause of it. Come on," he said, "let's go for a walk. Wait while I get my jacket."

"That reminds me. I never asked. Did they not have any new jackets in the shop?"

"What's that?" he called back from behind the door.

"The shop in Fort Angus. You were going to buy a new jacket."

"Oh, yes," he said, reappearing with a smile. "But they were all a bit too expensive. So where shall we go? Down to the harbor? Along the beach?"

Suddenly I had an idea.

"No," I said. "Let's go to Glasgow."

"Glasgow?"

"Yes! It's the weekend. I don't have to be back until Monday morning. We could stay with my friend."

"Anna, I don't think . . ."

"I can buy your bus ticket, if that's what you're worried about. And we'd get a sofa and a bit of floor to sleep on for free. Come on! A night out in Glasgow—that's exactly what I need. And then tomorrow you can show me all the places I should have seen years ago."

Just the thought of escaping Kilverbeg had cooled my anger. I couldn't wait.

"Andy does his afternoon run to Fort Angus at five o'clock," I continued. "We could be in Glasgow by eight. What do you think?"

"I think that we've just come *back* from Fort Angus. And I think that I don't have the money for a big night out. I don't have a job, remember?"

"I told you, I'll pay for you."

"Anna, I don't want to take your money."

"Right now, there's nothing else I'd like to spend it on. Let me buy your ticket. Come on, please! Don't make me go by myself!"

Cal paused. He was clearly hesitating.

"I'm sorry," he said at last. "It would be fun, but I just can't afford it. And I don't feel comfortable taking your money."

"OK," I said, thinking. I looked at my watch. "How about this then? It's just past three. Meet me at the harbor in one hour."

"Why?"

"You'll see. It'll be a surprise."

He smiled. "Alright," he said. "At four o'clock?"

"Four o'clock. And bring your coat."

Chapter 6

Growing closer

"What do you think?" I asked.

We were standing on the rocks above Ardbuchan Bay, only a few miles from Kilverbeg harbor. Below us, the small, empty beach was golden in the lowering sun.

"It's amazing," answered Cal.

"The perfect place for a picnic," I said. "I used to come here to swim when I was younger."

"Let's get a fire going," he said. He jumped down onto the sand and turned to offer me a hand.

"Do I look like I need your help?" I asked, laughing. With a single jump, I landed easily on the beach. "I hope you're hungry," I told him, opening my bag.

Half an hour later, we were sitting together around a fire as it fought back the cooling evening air. We had finished most of our picnic: pieces of cold chicken and sausages, some salad and cheeses, and some fruit.

"You see?" said Cal, smiling. "Who needs Glasgow?!"

"It's certainly cheaper staying here," I answered. "And it's exactly what I needed, to escape the village for a while. So thanks for coming."

"You don't need to thank me," Cal laughed. "I'm being very selfish, really, hiding you away from everyone else. Maybe we can go to Glasgow another time, but unfortunately . . ."

I stopped him talking with a kiss. When I pulled away a few seconds later, I could see even in the light of the fire that his face had turned red.

"That was a pleasant surprise," he said.

"Come on," I answered, standing up. "It's getting cold out here."

When we walked into the Hope and Anchor, Dad was already there. He was fast asleep, with his head on a table.

"What happened, Anna?" asked Mrs. Flannery, behind the bar. "Did you two have an argument? He's been in a terrible mood, but he wouldn't say what the matter was."

"It's nothing," I said, trying to wake him. "He's just tired." I knew that anything I told Mrs. Flannery would be all around the village by morning.

She didn't believe me for a second, but she smiled kindly. "He'll need to sleep. You won't get him home like that. If you want, you can take him upstairs. He can sleep in the spare room."

"Thank you."

With Cal's help, Dad was soon lying comfortably on a bed. I pulled off his boots, and we left him to sleep.

Half an hour later, we were sitting downstairs at a table in a corner of the pub again. It was so warm and comfortable that I was beginning to fall asleep myself. Maybe that's why I felt I could speak so directly.

"I've known you less than a week," I continued, looking at him closely. "But I feel like I know you so much better. Why is that?"

"We're similar people, I guess. We've similar backgrounds and similar ages . . ."

"How old are you, anyway?"

"Twenty-two. And you?"

I made a face. "Twenty. Twenty years, and I've still not escaped Kilverbeg."

"Why not? Why haven't you gone to college, or at least moved to work in Glasgow like all of your friends?"

"I had a place at college once."

"So why didn't you go?"

I took another drink and told him. "My mum. She was the local nurse here. She looked after everyone. Everyone loved her. She was a great nurse. She made everyone better. And when they were too sick or too old, she sat through the nights with them. She held their hands, and stayed with them until they died."

"So what happened?"

"She got ill herself. Cancer. It was a long and painful end. I was going to go to Glasgow, to study to be a nurse like her. But when she fell ill, I stayed to care for her. And then, when she died at last, I realized I couldn't leave Dad alone. He had already lost one of us."

"I'm sorry," said Cal. "But you'll get your chance to see the world, I'm sure."

"Maybe, one day," I said, and finished my drink. "And what about you? When did you leave Portrose for Glasgow?"

"A few years ago."

"And your father was a fisherman. What about your mother?"

"She worked beside him. They did everything together." Cal stood up and pointed at my empty glass. "Let me get you another drink."

As Cal stood by the bar waiting for Mrs. Flannery to pour us our drinks, he pulled his wallet out of his pocket. And then he took some money out of the wallet—a lot of money. I could see the notes clearly. It was at least two hundred pounds, more than enough for a bus ticket to Glasgow. And more than enough for a new jacket.

"I thought you said you didn't have much money," I said when he returned with the drinks. I pointed at the wallet in his pocket.

"No. I just said that I don't have money to spare."

"Yet Mrs. Black told me you paid her rent for a whole month."

"She wouldn't let me give her any less."

I sat watching him in silence. Suddenly, I felt more awake. Something didn't seem right.

Cal smiled at me, but it seemed forced and uncomfortable. "What's wrong?" he asked.

"I'm just thinking," I told him. "Every time I ask you about yourself, you're deliberately vague and then you change the subject."

"No, I don't!"

"You do. You did it again just then. I asked about your parents, and you almost ran to the bar."

"Anna, I went to buy more drinks!"

Something was wrong, but I couldn't tell what. I felt like I was looking for an answer to a question, but I couldn't yet work out what that question was.

"And the way you talk . . ." I said.

"What about it?"

"You speak like me."

Cal laughed. "So?"

"You say you only left Portrose a few years ago, but you sound like me. Your accent is from the west coast."

"I've been in Glasgow. That's on the west coast."

Suddenly it was clear. "That woman in Fort Angus! She *did* know you, didn't she? She wasn't from Portrose at all. You've been lying to me. You know this area, don't you?"

Cal said nothing. But his face told me everything. I was right.

Chapter 7

Still a stranger

"I don't believe it!" I said, my voice growing louder. "All this time, you've been lying to me."

"Anna! Calm down."

"Well? What are you going to tell me now? Another lie?"

For a while, Cal sat in silence. He seemed to be thinking carefully. And then, at last, he spoke.

"I'm sorry, Anna. I never wanted to lie to you. I like you, Anna. I really do. I never expected . . ." He stopped, and then seemed to try again. "You're right. I haven't been honest with you. Not completely. I did grow up in Portrose. That much is true. But I have been to this area once before. It was two years ago. Something terrible happened, something that I've tried to forget ever since. It changed my life forever. I came back to Argyll to try to overcome my past."

"What was it? What happened?"

He shook his head, and his voice was very quiet. "I can't tell you, Anna. I wish I could."

"You mean you don't want to tell me."

"That's right. Not yet anyway. You already mean too much to me."

I looked at him. And I could see the genuine pain in his eyes.

"I just need to deal with my past, and move forward," he said. "That's why I came to Kilverbeg, to deal with my past. I never expected to meet you."

He seemed so upset and so sincere that I could only feel pity. And, despite his sadness, I felt something like excitement too, because Cal had just confirmed his feelings for me.

I reached over and put my hand on his. "Tell me what happened. It might help to talk about it."

"I can't," he shook his head. "Maybe someday. But not yet."

I was curious, of course, but I understood. And at that moment, I just wanted him to know that. "It's OK," I told him. I moved round the table to sit beside him, and put my hand on his. "You can tell me when you feel ready. I can wait. I'd like to wait."

For a brief instant, I saw in his eyes once more the pain of whatever was tearing him up inside. It made me feel so sorry for him. I kissed him again, softly, and held his hand tighter. He smiled weakly and placed his other hand on top of mine. "Thank you," he said.

When I woke the next morning, Kilverbeg no longer seemed gray or lifeless. Even the dark clouds above the sea to the west seemed bright, like old friends. Dad was already in the kitchen when I walked in. He looked terrible, but he tried to hide it.

"I understand you were out last night with Cal," he said.

"So?" I replied, starting to make coffee.

"I'm not looking for an argument, Anna. I was just going to ask if you had a good evening."

I nodded. "Yes, I did. And I still don't know why you have such a problem with him."

"I don't have a problem with him! My problem is with you and your suggestion that I'm too old to do my job."

"I never said that. I just think it would be good for you to have some help, that's all."

Slowly, Dad stood up. "Anna," he said, "I don't have the energy for this conversation again." He moved toward the door. "I'm going to work."

Five minutes later, there was a knock at the door.

"Cal?" I called, already smiling as I opened it.

"Good morning, Anna." It was Donald. Despite it being a Sunday morning, he was wearing his police uniform. And he was looking very uncomfortable. "I'm sorry to be calling so early," he said. "Can I come in? I need to speak to you."

Puzzled, I nodded and stepped back. He followed me into the hall.

"What is it?" I asked. "What's wrong?"

"This is difficult for me, Anna, because I don't want to upset you. But there's something I have to tell you."

"What?"

"Anna, part of my job is to look after this village. It's a quiet place. I know it's a little too quiet for you at times. But I have a responsibility to keep it that way."

"So?"

"So if someone comes to stay in Kilverbeg without a job, without any family or friends in the village, I have to wonder why. I have to listen to what I hear people say and I have to do some investigating of my own. So I looked up your friend Callum Mackendry."

My heart suddenly started racing. I couldn't speak.

"I did a few checks on him," Donald continued. "And I found out something very alarming. He's been lying to you, Anna. He's been lying to all of us. Callum Mackendry isn't his real name."

Chapter 8

The truth revealed?

"That can't be right."

"Anna, I checked. He claims to be from Portrose, doesn't he?"

I nodded.

"No one called Callum Mackendry has ever lived in Portrose. In fact, there are only three people with that name in the whole of Glasgow. Two of them are over sixty, and the other is eight years old. Whoever your friend is, his name isn't Callum Mackendry."

I put a hand against the wall to hold myself steady. My head was beginning to ache.

"The official records don't lie, Anna. And I've checked them all."

"Why? Why have you been checking your records? What's he done wrong?"

"He's lied to you! Isn't that bad enough?"

"So maybe he did lie about Portrose. Maybe he lied about Glasgow. That doesn't mean he's not who he says he is. And even if you're right, what does it matter? It's not illegal to change your name. That doesn't mean he deserves to be investigated by the police!"

"Anna, he's pretending to be someone he's not!"

"Since when was that illegal?"

Donald sighed. "Of course it's not illegal. I'm not going to arrest him. I've no plans to even talk to him at the moment. But I wanted to let you know."

"Why? Why are you telling me this?"

"Anna, he's not being honest with you. Surely that should worry you. You've been spending a lot of time with him. That trip to Fort Angus, and then last night in the Hope . . ."

"I see. You've heard the talk around the village. Is that what this is about? I choose to go for a drink with him instead of you, so you start attacking him? You start using your police powers to make his life difficult?"

"Of course not. I just don't want to see you hurt."

"Well, I am hurt. I'm hurt that a friend like you could act this way."

"Anna, ask yourself this: what do you actually know about him? Why is he really in Kilverbeg? What's he hiding from?"

"I'd be the first person to ask why someone would want to come to Kilverbeg. But the fact that he has doesn't make him a criminal! You've no right to investigate someone who has done nothing wrong!"

"Anna . . ."

"I think you should leave now, Donald," I interrupted. I was very angry. He wasn't being fair to Cal.

With a silent nod, Donald turned and walked out of the house.

The headache was growing now. I felt terrible. But as I calmed, I began to think. Perhaps Donald had been wrong to investigate Cal. But right or wrong, that didn't change what he had discovered. Cal—or whatever his real name was—had lied to me. Again.

It was almost eight o'clock, and it was growing windy outside. Picking up my jacket, I began walking to Cal's flat. As I went, I thought more about what he had told me. He had said that something had happened two years before, something terrible that he had tried to forget. And he had returned to the area to try to overcome his past.

If he hadn't wanted to tell me more, that was his choice. I respected that. But I wanted him to respect me as well. I wanted him to be honest about the things he did tell me. And obviously, if Donald was right, he wasn't being honest.

"Cal!" I shouted, banging on his door. "Cal! I need to speak to you."

There was no answer.

As my headache grew worse, I grew angrier. I started banging harder.

"Cal! Are you in there?"

Still no answer. He was obviously out. But then the door moved slightly. Without really thinking what I was doing, I pushed again, and it opened. Because of the broken lock, he must have thought it was properly closed when it was only stuck.

"Cal?" I called again, but it was clear that he wasn't there.

I was about to pull the door properly shut again when I hesitated. However uncomfortable I felt at the idea, I now had a chance to find out more about him. I knew it was wrong, to go into his flat without him, and I wanted him to trust me. But he had lied to me. So shaking off my feelings of guilt, I stepped inside.

The place was quite dark, and it was surprisingly tidy. I began to look around. It seemed like Cal had very few possessions of his own. The living room was empty, and there was only a little food in the kitchen fridge. There were a few clothes in the bedroom cupboard. On top was a small piece of leather. I picked it up, and recognized what it was immediately. It was a cover for a fisherman's knife. The cover protects the knife from the salt water and keeps it sharp. My dad had one just like it. The knife is useful for cutting the ropes on nets, especially when they're tied too tightly to unwrap. If a net gets caught, it can be very dangerous for everyone on the boat, and a sharp knife can make all the difference.

I held the knife cover up toward the light of the window. There were two letters cut into the leather: "MB." MB? Could they be the initials of Cal's real name? So, a knife cover, but where was the knife?

It was as I was returning the cover to the shelf that I saw the large envelope under the clothes. It was made of cardboard, and it was a little dirty, as if someone had handled it a lot. Inside were lots of pieces of paper. One was a map of the coast; it showed Kilverbeg and all the other surrounding villages and islands. Most of the villages had a line of ink through their names—perhaps they were places that Cal had already tried to find work. Beneath the map was a notebook full of writing. And beside that was a page from a newspaper. Holding it close to the window, I began to read.

> "*Accident at sea,*" read the story. "*Two people died last night when their fishing boat was destroyed. The accident happened after dark just three miles from the coast of Argyll, less than a mile south of the Black Rocks. Police think the most likely explanation is that the boat exploded as a result of a faulty engine. However, they are also investigating the possibility that another boat was involved. Inspector Danielli of the Glasgow office is managing the investigation. 'It's possible that these deaths were the result of two boats crashing together in the dark,' he said this morning. 'We would like to speak to anyone who was out at sea in that area as soon as possible.'*"

With shaking hands, I looked in the corner of the page for the newspaper date. I already knew what I would see. It was dated two years before.

Suddenly, I understood the significance of the story, and why Cal had kept it. He had talked about something two years before that had changed his life, something terrible. And this was it. Cal must have been the fisherman who caused the crash. Cal was responsible for two deaths. And he had taken a new name and come to Kilverbeg to hide from his crime.

Chapter 9

The real threat

I had found what I was looking for. I had found out who Cal really was. Suddenly, it all made sense. It was no surprise that he had lied about his real name.

Quickly, I folded the paper and returned it to its hiding place. Then I left the flat, pulling the door tightly shut behind me. As I walked home, the rain fell on my face so hard it almost hurt, and my mind felt as wild as the wind.

I needed to think. My headache was growing worse. But I had to make a decision. I had to decide whether or not I should tell Donald what I had discovered.

Cal was responsible for killing two people, and surely he had to pay for that. Didn't the families of those two people have a right to know what had really happened? Didn't they have the right to see Cal face the consequences according to law?

But what good would that do? It had been an accident, not intentional. The legal system couldn't bring those two poor people back to life. And could it really make Cal feel worse than he already did? I knew that he was upset by what he had done. I had seen that clearly, and heard it in his words. And although he may have lied to me, there was still something between us that was honest. I felt certain of that. He had told me how he felt about me, and I couldn't deny my feelings for him. He had brought a new happiness into my life. Was I going to pay him back by reporting him to the police?

I didn't know what to do. Perhaps Donald would discover Cal's real name soon anyway, even if I said nothing. Or maybe the police had already stopped looking for anyone. There was only one way to find out. I knew I couldn't ask Donald, so I looked up the number and picked up the phone. Sixty miles away in Glasgow, someone answered.

"Can I speak to Inspector Danielli, please?" I asked.

"You mean Chief Inspector Danielli. Can I ask who's calling, please?"

"My name is Anna Cross. I'm calling from Kilverbeg. It's important."

"One moment, please."

A few seconds later, a deep voice answered the phone. "This is Danielli."

"Chief Inspector, I'm sorry to bother you. I was wondering if I could ask you a few questions about an old investigation of yours. It was two years ago. Two people were killed when their boat was destroyed, near the Black Rocks."

"I remember."

"Was anyone ever caught?"

"It was an accident, that's all. Just very bad luck. There was a problem with the engine and it started a fire. It's rare, but it happens."

"Did you ever recover the boat? Were you able to prove that it was an engine fault?"

"No. The boat was destroyed."

"Then how do you know that no other boats were involved? Were you not investigating that as a possibility at one time?"

"That's correct. But no one ever believed it was a serious possibility. You see, you would need a much larger boat to destroy a small fishing boat like that. And all fishing boats over fifteen metres are fitted with satellite recorders, so we were able to check the records. There were no other boats in the area at that time. We also checked to see if any boats had been reported as damaged. If it had been a crash, even a larger boat would have shown some signs of damage. We didn't find any. So we were able to say with confidence that it was a fault with the engine."

"So the case is now closed?"

"That's right. Which makes me wonder why you're asking about it. You're not a friend of the family, are you? They were from near Kilverbeg. Did you know them?"

"No," I said, ready with my excuse. "I'm writing a story about the accident, and just wanted to check some details."

"Well, if you want to make it a good story, you should speak to their son."

"Whose son?"

"The son of the couple who died."

"They were a husband and wife?"

Chief Inspector Danielli cleared his throat. "You haven't really done much research yet, have you? Yes, they were a husband and wife. Angus and Emma Blair. Their son Michael was in the boat with them, but he was asleep at the time. He was thrown into the water and knocked his head. When he woke up several hours later, after he was rescued, he insisted that he'd seen another fishing boat. That's the only reason we had to investigate it."

I was finding it hard to speak.

"Hello?" said Danielli. "Are you still there?"

"The son," I managed to say. "Michael. How old was he?"

"I forget exactly. Perhaps about twenty. The poor boy never really got over it. He bothered us for months afterwards. He moved to Glasgow, and was always here at the station asking us what we were doing to find that other boat. Even though he was asleep

throughout the whole thing, he refused to believe he could have imagined it. In fact, he only stopped bothering us a few weeks ago. Ms. Cross? Hello? Ms. Cross?"

Hardly able to breathe, I hung up the telephone. I didn't need to hear any more. I had discovered who Cal really was. His name was Michael Blair. And he wasn't a killer; he was a victim.

But what was he doing in Kilverbeg? And why was he trying to keep his identity a secret? The answers came to me slowly, through the pain of my headache. Cal—or Michael—was looking for a fishing boat that showed signs of damage from two years before. He was looking for someone who, two years before, had taken that boat out to sea. He was looking for the person he believed had killed his parents. He was looking for my dad.

Chapter 10

Too late?

The more I thought about it, the more I understood. Michael—I would have to start calling him that—believed that another boat was responsible for killing his parents. And because Michael knew the area, he must have known the few fishing villages nearby. Perhaps he had already visited them to look for the person who killed his parents. And then he came to Kilverbeg, and he found my dad.

Even two years ago, Dad was the only person still fishing out of the village. And I had told Michael about the damage to his boat myself! He must have thought the story about hitting the harbor wall was just an excuse to explain the damage.

But Danielli had been clear. The police had checked all the satellite recorders and there were no fishing boats in the area that night. So Dad couldn't have been involved. And besides, even without the satellite evidence, I knew Dad wasn't a killer. So why did Michael refuse to believe the police? Had his sadness and loss stopped him from thinking properly?

Whatever the answer, I had to warn Dad. I didn't know what Michael was going to do to him, but it couldn't be good. I thought of the empty knife cover in Mrs. Black's flat, and I felt sick.

Picking up my jacket, I ran out into the rain. A storm was coming. I hurried through the wind toward the water as fast as I could.

I arrived at the harbor with a sigh of relief. Dad's boat wasn't there. That meant he was out at sea. He was safe. He probably wouldn't be back until the end of the day at the earliest. That gave me plenty of time to think what to do.

"Are you looking for your father?"

I turned. Mrs. Flannery was walking past, on her way to the Hope and Anchor.

I nodded and tried to smile. "I just wanted to ask him something before he went. But it doesn't matter."

"I hope it wasn't important. They might not be back for hours. Although the way he was last night, he should still be in bed."

"They?"

"Yes. He went out with Callum, the boy you were with last night. That's nice for you, isn't it, that they get on so well together? In all these years, I can't remember when your dad last took someone else fishing with him."

"You're sure? Dad took Cal with him?"

"Of course I'm sure. That's my front window just up there. I saw them leave."

I couldn't believe it. Dad had taken Michael out on his boat, and it was all my fault! I had told him to give Michael some work. I had bothered him about it until he gave in. Now Dad was helpless. He had no idea who Michael really was, or what he believed. He was alone at sea with a man who wanted to do him harm.

I had to warn him. That meant I had to find a radio, and quickly. Only a hundred yards away along the beach was the lifeboat station. There was a radio in there.

I hurried over and ran inside to the office. Two seconds later, I was calling Dad.

"*Bella Anna, Bella Anna, Bella Anna*, this is Kilverbeg Coast Guard on channel sixteen. Over."

I took my finger off the button and waited for the reply. A few seconds later, I tried again.

"Bella Anna, Bella Anna, this is Kilverbeg Coast Guard. Please respond. Over."

There was no answer. Dad always answered his radio, always. I had to find them. I had to convince Michael that he was wrong. Without any further thought, I prepared the lifeboat and, a few minutes later, was starting the engine and heading out into the storm.

I had just passed the harbor when the radio came to life.

"Anna? Anna! Is that you?"

It was Donald.

"Anna? I'm watching our lifeboat head out to sea. Tell me that's not you in it, all by yourself!"

"Donald!" I answered. "This is an emergency. I need your help. You were right about Cal. That's not his real name. His real name is Michael Blair. His parents were killed in an accident two years ago when their engine exploded. But Michael thinks that Dad had something to do with it. They're out in the *Bella Anna*. Donald, I think he's going to do something to Dad."

There was only a brief pause, and then Donald's voice returned. *"What do you want me to do?"*

"I need to know where they've gone, and I can't get through on Dad's radio. Contact the National Fishing Satellite Centre. Ask them to use the boat's satellite recorder to find them."

"Anna, what are you going to do? You're not even meant to be in that lifeboat by yourself. How are you going to stop Cal, or Michael, even if you find him?"

"Please, Donald. Just do it!"

There was another pause. Then Donald replied. *"Give me two minutes."*

It was at least five minutes before I heard his voice again. All that time, I just pointed the boat straight out to sea.

"Anna? Anna, are you there?"

"Go ahead."

"It doesn't make sense. According to his satellite recorder, your dad's boat is in the harbor."

"What?!" I wasn't sure if I had heard Donald right above the noise of the storm.

"I said there's something wrong. According to the satellite equipment, the Bella Anna *isn't even at sea!"*

It wasn't hard to guess what had happened. Michael must have broken Dad's satellite recorder so no one could follow them.

"Anna? What are you going to do?"

I thought carefully. Michael had obviously thought about this day for a long time. So what was he planning? Where had he taken Dad?

And then I realized. There was only one possible answer. Michael wanted Dad to pay for the death of his parents. He wanted to bring an end to his hunt in the very place it had started. Turning the boat into the wind, I pushed it as fast as the storm would allow toward the Black Rocks, the place where Michael's parents had died.

Chapter 11

Into the storm

As I fought to push the boat through the high waves, I just had to hope that I would find them in time. And I couldn't help thinking about Michael. Had he been using me from the start? Is that how he knew Dad's last name when I introduced the two men, not because he had been asking people in the village about me, but because he'd been asking about Dad? Was Michael only pretending to like me to get close to my dad?

The lifeboat was fast, much faster than Dad's fishing boat. Within fifteen minutes, I could see the *Bella Anna*. It was less than a hundred yards west of the Black Rocks. The boat was rolling dangerously in the waves. The engine didn't seem to be working. I could see the two men on the top of the boat. Dad was on his knees and Michael was standing over him. They were both holding tight to the rails, and shouting at each other above the wind.

Neither of them had noticed me. If Michael was really planning to kill my dad, I had to make sure he knew that I was there as soon as possible. That way, Michael would know that he could never blame my dad's death on an accident. He would realize that he could never escape with murder. But then, I thought, perhaps he wasn't planning to escape.

Minutes later I was beside them. The waves were too big to get close enough to tie the lifeboat to the *Bella Anna*. And I couldn't get close enough to be heard by shouting. I picked up the lifeboat's loudspeaker and turned it on.

"Michael!" I called. My voice carried easily through the storm. "I know who you are. And I know what you think. But you're wrong. You're wrong!"

Slowly, Cal turned toward me. It was then that I saw what was in his hand: his fishing knife. He was holding it tight and pointing it at Dad.

He paused for a moment, looking me straight in the eye across the water, and then he shook his head. His message was clear: "No," he was saying. "I'm not wrong."

"I spoke to the police," I tried again through the loudspeaker. "I spoke to Chief Inspector Danielli. He's certain. They checked all the satellite recorders. No other boats were near here on the night that your parents died."

Cal didn't try to answer me. Instead, he shouted something at Dad and waved the knife. Whatever it was that Michael said, it made Dad turn slowly round toward me. His face was low. I couldn't see it at first. But then, slowly, as though it was the last thing in the world that he wanted to do, he looked at me.

And in that instant, I saw the truth in Dad's face. He didn't need to say anything. With just a look, I knew that Michael was right. Somehow, Dad *had* been involved.

I froze in shock, and the loudspeaker fell from my hand. I couldn't believe it. But Dad couldn't have been clearer if he had spoken the words. My own father was somehow responsible for the death of Cal's parents.

Michael saw the look on my face. He knew that I had at last understood the truth. And then he stepped toward Dad, still holding the knife. Suddenly, it was clear: he wasn't thinking about escape. He just wanted to make sure Dad paid for what he had done.

There was nothing I could do but watch. "No!" I shouted. But I knew as soon as I spoke that the wind stole my shout away. Michael moved closer still. He bent down and shouted something in Dad's ear. And then he raised the knife.

"Please!" I heard myself say.

BELLA ANNA

At that moment, Michael turned his face to mine. He looked a picture of sadness, but also strangely calm. It was as if he had finished something important. And then, slowly drawing back his arm, he threw the knife into the water. It disappeared immediately beneath the waves.

I couldn't believe it. Michael *wasn't* going to kill Dad. In fact, as I watched, I saw him reach out to help Dad to his feet. And that's when the *Bella Anna* hit the rocks.

At first, I didn't understand what was happening. The fishing boat seemed to jump in the water. None of us had noticed that the wind had pushed us toward the Black Rocks. The *Bella Anna* was between me and the rocks, so the lifeboat was fine. But Dad's boat had suffered badly. It came to rest in an odd position.

And that's when I noticed that Dad had disappeared. And Michael was looking over the side of the boat, searching the sea. Before I could do anything, he had used a rope to tie a lifebelt to his body and stepped over the rails. Then, with only a quick look toward me, he threw the lifebelt into the water and jumped in after it.

Immediately, I picked up the radio and called the emergency alarm. "Mayday," I called. "Mayday, mayday. This is Kilverbeg Coast Guard. I say again, Kilverbeg Coast Guard. Fishing boat *Bella Anna* has hit the Black Rocks. The boat is taking on water. Both crew are in the water. Repeat: two men are in the water. This is the Kilverbeg Coast Guard. Requesting immediate help at the Black Rocks."

As the waves pushed and pulled the lifeboat, it was difficult to control. I had to avoid the rocks yet stay as close as possible. And all the time, I was looking anxiously around, desperate for some sign of Dad. I could see the orange lifebelt disappearing and then reappearing behind each wave, and Michael swimming again and again under the surface. But each time he came back up alone.

"Dad!" I screamed. I felt helpless. Even if Dad was on the surface, the waves were rising and falling. They would be hiding him from my view. It was hopeless.

Then I noticed that the lifebelt was sitting freely on the waves by itself. It was no longer attached to Michael, but just sitting on an otherwise empty sea. And, beyond, the *Bella Anna* was sinking.

That's when I heard my name. "Anna!"

I turned. There, on the other side of the lifeboat, was Michael. And beside him in the water, swimming weakly with Michael's help, was Dad. I could see a big cut on the top of his head, where he must have knocked it against his ship as it hit the rocks.

"Dad!" I shouted, and ran over to the side of the lifeboat. Moments later, Michael was pushing and I was pulling him in. Dad was wet through, bleeding and exhausted, but he was safe.

I turned back to the boat's edge to help Michael. And that's when I saw the wave.

Before, the lifeboat had protected him from the worst of the wind. But there on the other side of the boat, the waves were even bigger. And one particular wave was rushing toward us. It was enormous, and it was fast.

Before I could do anything, it was on us. It picked Michael up and threw him against the side of the lifeboat. As the whole boat rolled dangerously, I couldn't do anything but just hold on. And when the wave had passed and I looked back, Michael was gone.

The top of the *Bella Anna* was now close to the water line. And as I continued to search the sea for any sign of Michael, Dad watched his boat slip beneath the waves.

Chapter 12

Past or future

"Take the wheel," I shouted to Dad. Then, holding on tight, I climbed to the highest point on the lifeboat so that I could look all around for Michael. But it was useless. The storm was getting worse. In every direction, the waves were growing bigger. Dad and I exchanged a look. We both knew there was no hope.

At that moment, a Coast Guard helicopter appeared above our heads. The noise of the wind had hidden its approach. As it came closer to the water, a man lowered himself on a line, disappearing behind the waves. I couldn't see what was happening. And then, at last, the line pulled him higher again.

And another person was attached. It was Michael! I could see him moving his arms as he rose into the helicopter. He was safe.

"Kilverbeg Coast Guard, Kilverbeg Coast Guard. This is Fort Angus Sea Rescue. We received your message. We have pulled a man from the water. He seems OK. Do you have the other man?"

"We do," I replied. "Thank you. All are safe."

"No problem. Returning to base. Safe home."

With a wave at the helicopter as it flew over our heads toward the coast, I turned the lifeboat toward Kilverbeg.

◇◇◇

Two hours later, I was sitting by Michael's bed at Fort Angus hospital when he woke up.

"How are you feeling?" I asked.

His smile was unconvincing. "Like I'll never be properly dry again."

"The doctor wants to keep you here for a few days, but he says you'll be fine."

There was an uncomfortable silence.

"Michael," I said, "Dad wants to talk to you."

At my words, he turned his face away toward the wall. But he didn't stop me when I stood and walked to the door, to where Donald was waiting in the corridor. "Can you send Dad through?" I asked.

A moment later, Dad walked slowly into the room. He had a large dressing over the cut on his head, and he looked terrible. He looked older and smaller than I had ever seen him.

He stood at the bottom of Michael's bed with his head hanging low. In silence, he stared at the bed sheets. For a long time, the room was perfectly still. The only sound was the noise of the hospital lights.

"Michael," said Dad at last, and then immediately stopped. He swallowed, and tried again. "Michael?"

Michael's face was still turned to the wall. It was impossible to see his expression.

"I can't . . . I can't tell you how sorry I am, Michael. Or how ashamed I am. It was . . ."

I could see the tears gathering in Dad's eyes as he took a deep breath. Then, with his eyes still fixed on the bottom of the bed, he forced himself to continue.

"It was all over before I knew what was happening. By the time I stopped the engine . . . It was so dark. I told myself it was just a piece of wood, just . . ."

Still Michael refused to turn and look at Dad.

"The next morning, I heard all about it. And I knew what I had done." Dad stopped again. In the silence, I could hear Michael starting to cry. But Dad didn't stop. It was as though he had to get the words out, like he had been waiting to say them for a long time.

"I convinced myself it would do no good to tell the police. It wouldn't bring your parents back. And I couldn't leave Anna alone; she had only just lost her mother. So I . . . I took the *Bella Anna* out the next morning and sailed it straight into the harbor wall, to hide any sign of damage."

Dad's eyes were red with tears as he finally looked up from the bed toward Michael. "Nothing I can say will ever make it right. I just want you to know how truly, truly sorry I am."

There was a long silence as we waited for Michael to react. But still he lay turned to the wall. I had no idea what he was thinking.

"Michael?" I said.

At last, he turned and sat up. For what seemed like several minutes but must have only been seconds, he stared at Dad, slowly wiping the tears from his face. And then he turned to me.

"I tried to keep this simple," he said. "I tried . . . I tried to ignore you."

I said nothing, but I thought of that moment on the bus to Fort Angus, when he had seen me and wanted to get off again.

"For the first time since Mum and Dad died," he continued, "you made me forget what happened." He reached out and took my hand in his. "They would have liked you, Anna. And not just because of what you've done for me."

Finally, Michael looked back at Dad. "It's true, isn't it," he said, "sometimes loving really does mean letting go."

I was holding Michael so tight and crying so hard that I didn't even hear Dad leave.

By the time Donald knocked on our front door the next morning, the storm had passed. For once, the sun was even shining.

"I wanted to let you both know as soon as I heard," he said, looking from Dad to me. "Thanks to Michael, there'll be no charges over the accident."

I turned to Dad with a smile as he lowered himself slowly into a kitchen chair. There were tears in his eyes.

"That's wonderful news," I said. "Thank you, Donald."

"However," he continued, stepping further into the room, "there's still the issue of the illegal fishing. Removing your satellite recorder from your boat is a serious crime, Mr. Cross. I understand your feelings about it. You know I do. And I've done all I can to defend you. But it is the law. There will be a fine to pay in punishment."

Dad nodded. "I understand," he said quietly.

"One last thing," said Donald, pulling an envelope from his jacket pocket and handing it to Dad. "You'll need these details when you come to make your insurance claim for the *Bella Anna*."

"Thank you, Donald, for everything."

As Donald drove away, I walked back into the kitchen. Dad hadn't moved. He was still sitting at the table, just staring at the envelope.

"What is it?" I asked. "Are you worried about the fine?"

"No," Dad shook his head. "The insurance will cover that."

"Then what's wrong?"

"I was just thinking . . . After I've paid the fine, there'll be more than enough left over to send you on your way."

"What do you mean?"

Dad looked up at me from the table. "Michael was right, Anna, when he talked about loving and letting go. Every child has a duty to their parents, but we also have a duty to live our own lives. I know you're only here in Kilverbeg for my sake. And I've been selfish in letting that continue. It's time for you to do what you always wanted. I love you, Anna, but it's time for me to let you go."

As I put my arms around him, I found I was smiling and crying at the same time. He held me tight.

"I'll be fine," he said to me. "It's time I retired anyway. You should go and find whatever it is you're looking for." He looked into my face and smiled. "And you might want to start in Fort Angus hospital."

Review: Chapters 1–4

A. Match the characters in the story to their descriptions.

1. ______ Anna Cross	**a.** The new arrival in the village
2. ______ Mrs. Black	**b.** The local bus driver
3. ______ Andy Bruce	**c.** The last fisherman in Kilverbeg
4. ______ Stuart Cross	**d.** The person who delivers the post
5. ______ Callum Mackendry	**e.** The person who runs the village shop

B. Read each statement and circle whether it is true (T) or false (F).

1. Anna loves Kilverbeg and wants to live there forever. T / F

2. Mrs. Black's rented flat is in perfect condition. T / F

3. Cal used to be a fisherman. T / F

4. Cal has come to live in Kilverbeg for three years. T / F

5. Stuart is happy to have a satellite recorder on his boat. T / F

6. Donald likes Anna very much. T / F

7. Stuart has never crashed his fishing boat. T / F

8. Anna normally loves the journey to Fort Angus. T / F

C. Choose the best answer for each question.

1. The first time Anna visits Cal, it's because ______.
a. her van is broken
b. she has a letter for him
c. she's curious
d. Mrs. Black has a message for him

2. Anna thinks that Kilverbeg is ______.
a. a great place to meet people
b. a boring place to live
c. too hot in the summer
d. too close to Glasgow

3. Cal says he has come to the village ______.
a. to look for a house to buy
b. to see his grandmother
c. because he's traveling around Scotland
d. because he's lost

Review: Chapters 5–8

A. Match the characters in the story to their descriptions.

1. What is Anna's plan that will allow Cal to stay in Kilverbeg? _____
2. Why does Donald come to Anna's house? _____
3. What does Anna do instead of going to Glasgow? _____
4. Why doesn't Stuart want to give Cal a job? _____
5. What does Anna see in Cal's room, marked with initials? _____
6. What does Anna understand from the newspaper story? _____

a. He can't afford to.
b. She learns that Cal was responsible for two deaths.
c. She has a picnic with Cal on the beach.
d. She discovers a leather cover for a knife.
e. He wants to reveal the truth to her about Cal.
f. She's going to ask her dad to give Cal a job.

B. Number these events in the order they happened (1–6).

_____ Donald knocks on Anna's front door.
_____ Anna and Cal put Stuart to bed.
_____ Stuart leaves for work after an argument with Anna.
_____ Anna looks around Cal's flat.
_____ Anna tries to get Cal to tell her about his past.
_____ Anna and Cal share their first kiss.

C. Complete the summary using words from the box.

argument	deaths	fishermen	help
lying	newspaper	picnic	truth

Anna wants Cal to work for her dad, but Stuart tells her he doesn't need any **1.** _____________. They have a(n) **2.** _____________, and Anna leaves to have a(n) **3.** _____________ with Cal by the sea. That evening, they're sitting in the pub when Anna realizes that Cal isn't telling her the whole **4.** _____________ about himself. The next morning, Hamish confirms that Cal has been **5.** _____________ to her. Anna looks around Cal's flat, to find out more about him. She finds a(n) **6.** _____________ suggesting that Cal was involved in the **7.** _____________ of two innocent **8.** _____________.

D. Complete the crossword.

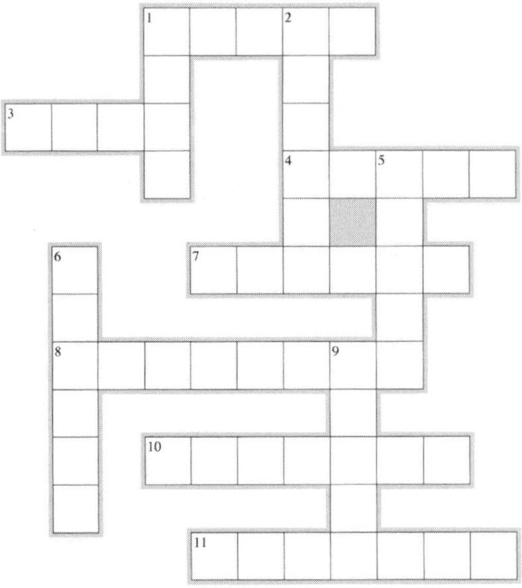

Across

1. The newspaper story tells of an accident near the ______ Rocks.
3. Kilverbeg's pub is called the ______ and Anchor.
4. Anna realizes that Cal's accent is from the west ______.
7. Cal and Anna agree to meet at the ______ at four o'clock.
8. Anna finds a large ______ under a pile of Cal's clothes.
10. Even though it's Sunday, Hamish wears his full police ______.
11. Anna sees that Cal has more than two ______ pounds in his wallet.

Down

1. Anna cooks a ______ pie for her dad.
2. Stuart's wife (Anna's mother) died of ______.
5. Stuart has always worked ______.
6. Anna is ______ years old.
9. Anna thinks Stuart is too ______ to agree to having help at work.

Review: Chapters 9–12

A. Choose the correct ending for each sentence.

1. Anna calls Chief Inspector Danielli to **(a)** *find out what they know about Cal* / **(b)** *tell the police what she has discovered.*

2. Anna realizes that Cal has really come to Kilverbeg to **(a)** *hide* / **(b)** *find Stuart.*

3. By the time Anna arrives at the harbor, Cal has already **(a)** *gone fishing with Stuart* / **(b)** *gone to speak to Donald.*

4. Anna goes out in the lifeboat **(a)** *with Donald* / **(b)** *by herself.*

5. Stuart's head is bleeding because **(a)** *he hit his head against the ship* / **(b)** *Cal cut him with the knife.*

6. Stuart plans to use the insurance money to **(a)** *buy a new boat* / **(b)** *send Anna traveling.*

B. Choose the best answer for each question.

1. Chief Inspector Danielli believes that ______.
   a. Anna is related to the fishermen who died
   b. Anna shouldn't get involved
   c. Cal's parents died in an accident
   d. Stuart should stop fishing

2. Anna thinks the *Bella Anna* will be at the Black Rocks because ______.
   a. she has heard about it on the radio
   b. the satellite recorder has told her where the boat is
   c. Stuart has told her that's where he's going fishing
   d. she knows that's where Cal's parents were killed

3. Stuart comes to talk to Cal in Fort Angus hospital because ______.
   a. he wants to apologize
   b. he's angry with Cal
   c. he wants to know if Cal is ill
   d. Anna tells him he has to

C. Match each question with the correct answer.

1. Who reveals to Anna the names of the two people who died? ______

2. Who tells Anna that her father has gone fishing with someone else? ______

3. Who rescues Stuart from the sea? ______

4. Who gives Stuart the report he needs for his insurance claim? ______

a. Mrs. Flannery

b. Chief Inspector Danielli

c. Donald

d. Cal

Answer Key

Chapters 1–4

A:

1. d; **2.** e; **3.** b; **4.** c; **5.** a

B:

1. F; **2.** F; **3.** T; **4.** F; **5.** F; **6.** T; **7.** F; **8.** F

C:

1. c; **2.** b; **3.** c

Chapters 5–8

A:

1. f; **2.** e; **3.** c; **4.** a; **5.** d; **6.** b

B:

5, 2, 4, 6, 3, 1

C:

help; argument; picnic; truth; lying; newspaper; deaths; fishermen

D:

Across

1. Black; **3.** Hope; **4.** coast; **7.** harbor; **8.** envelope; **10.** uniform; **11.** hundred

Down

1. beef; **2.** cancer; **5.** alone; **6.** twenty; **9.** proud

Chapters 9–12

A:

1. a; **2.** b; **3.** a; **4.** b; **5.** a; **6.** b

B:

1. c; **2.** d; **3.** a

C:

1. b; **2.** a; **3.** d; **4.** c

Background Reading:

Spotlight on . . . The Scottish Coast

Scotland is less than 450 km in length from north to south, but stretches to 10,000 km if you count the coasts of nearly 800 islands around it. This includes the St. Kilda islands in the Outer Hebrides, which form the furthest part of the British Isles.

Scotland boasts some spectacular natural landscapes, particularly on the west coast. This includes the Isle of Skye, the Inner and Outer Hebrides, and the remote and windy island of Jura, where George Orwell wrote his novel *1984*. Peaceful lakes, known as lochs, are common throughout the country. The most famous of these is Loch Ness, where the famous monster Nessie is said to live.

The coastal areas of Scotland are rich sources of energy. The land under the sea near Aberdeen, for example, contains large pockets of gas and oil. Intense winds and waves also support a growing industry in wind and tidal energy.

Scotland is also one of the largest sea-fishing nations in Europe. However, concerns over declining fish populations have led to calls from environmentalists and scientists to restrict fishing in the seas off the Scottish coast.

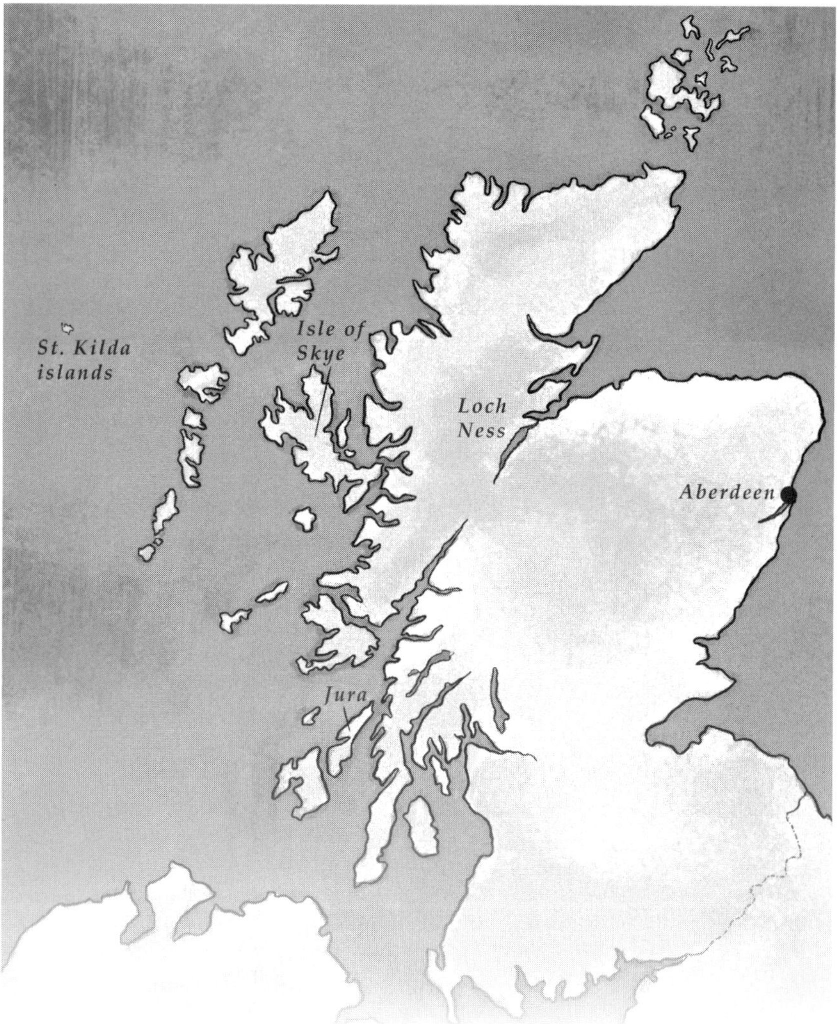

Think About It

1. Why do you think the west coast has a very different outline from the east coast?
2. Can you think of other industries that depend on the sea? Which of these are important in coastal areas closest to where you live?

Glossary

bay	(*n.*)	part of a coast where the land curves inwards
cancer	(*n.*)	a serious disease in which abnormal body cells increase, producing growths
harbor	(*n.*)	an area of water which is partly enclosed by land or strong walls, so that boats can be left there safely
loch	(*n.*)	the Irish and Scottish Gaelic term for a lake or a sea inlet.
loudspeaker	(*n.*)	a device that changes electrical signals into sounds loud enough to be heard at a distance
pub	(*n.*)	bars serving drinks and food, commonly found in the United Kingdom
quiz	(*n.*)	a test, game, or competition in which someone tests your knowledge by asking questions
rope	(*n.*)	a thick cord or wire made by twisting together several thinner cords/wires
satellite	(*n.*)	an object in space which collects information or is part of a communications system